TELL ME ABOUT
Hinduism

TELL ME ABOUT
Hinduism

VANEETA VAID

Nita Mehta
Enriching Young Minds

TELL ME ABOUT
Hinduism

3rd Print 2010

ISBN 978-81-7676-037-9

Illustrations:  Nita Mehta
Enriching Young Minds

Layout and laser typesetting:

 National Information
Technology Academy
3A/3, Asaf Ali Road
New Delhi-110002
N.I.T.A. ☎ 23252948

Contributing Writers :
Anurag Mehta
Subhash Mehta

Editorial & Proofreading :
Rakesh
Ramesh

Printed at:
MEHTA OFFSET

Distributed by:
NITA MEHTA BOOKS
3A/3, Asaf Ali Road,
New Delhi - 110 002
Tel: 23250091, 23252948
Email: nitamehta@nitamehta.com

Price: Rs. 295/-

Published by:

Nita Mehta
Enriching Young Minds

3A/3 Asaf Ali Road, New Delhi-110002
Tel: 91-11-23250091, 29214011, 23252948, 29218727
Fax: 91-11-29225218
E-Mail : nitamehta@email.com
nitamehta@nitamehta.com
Website : http://www.nitamehta.com,
http://www.snabindia.com

Contents

Why a book on HINDUISM?

Every child has a natural curiosity to know and understand the various facets of life. This holds true for religion as well. His young mind is constantly looking for answers to questions like:

- *"Who created the Universe?"*

- *"What or who is God?"*

The imparting of spiritual knowledge and moral values through normal teaching methods can be very boring for children! However, the importance of this knowledge cannot be dismissed. Many of us have been faced with the query - *"Where have ethics and moral values vanished, along with depleting forests and environment?"* To restore these, we need to inculcate strong moral values in children.

As adults, even though we may have forgotten many of the scientific and mathematical theories and applications we learnt in school, the values inculcated in us by our parents can never be eroded. To inculcate such values, we need to develop means and tools which could be used to facilitate such learning. Towards this objective, we present this book.

Sincere efforts have been made to make an easy, illustrative work of interesting stories about creation, spiritualism and moral values for children! The book has been designed to give children a complete know-how about Hinduism in a simple and colourful way. What was spoken millions of years ago about faith and religion, makes so much of sense even today! We believe that this book is a must read for children and a good buy for parents who want their children to know what the great religion - Hinduism - is all about.

What is Hinduism?

Hinduism is one of the world's oldest religions which began in India more than 5,000 years ago. What exactly does religion mean? Religion is a system of faith and worship by humans towards a personal God or Gods. Without the guidance of religion, our lives would be in chaos and there would be no rules of good or bad!

Hinduism is a faith, belief, philosophy of thoughts and conviction, largely followed by the people of **India** and the people of the small Himalayan kingdom of **Nepal**. It is called the religion of these countries. The followers of this religion are called **Hindus**. Hinduism is followed in many countries though over two-thirds of its followers live in India.

Some believe Hinduism is as old as the earth! Let us recognize from the beginning, the beliefs of this faith. How it began and how it has grown into such a strong force that has become the third largest religion in the world having over 500 million followers?

The Beginning

Vishnu orders Brahma to create the world

Creation of the World, (Western interpretation)...

Astronomer Edwin Hubble proved that billions of years ago an outer space explosion caused a big bang that threw material or matter in all directions creating the Universe! He said space, galaxies, the solar system including the earth, was very scientifically created!

What Hinduism Says...

Some legends or fables from Hinduism have another story to tell. Their story is: Billions of years ago, there was no universe, no space, no earth! Only an endless dark emptiness, between vast oceans! In all this nothingness, there lived a serpent called **Sheshnaag**. This serpent rode on the waves of the ocean forever! Then, something happened and everything changed. Whilst the serpent lay curled on the waters, from deep down somewhere, a noise vibrated. The noise sounded like: "OM-MMMMMMMM"! It filled the emptiness and rang into the black darkness. You know what this noise was? It was the first hum of sound! The darkness began to go away breaking into the first rays of light, which meant finally dawn had come! Sheshnaag stirred and from inside his coils emerged **Lord Vishnu**. From Lord Vishnu's navel, grew a lotus flower! It flowered and bloomed! Within the lotus, sat someone else. Who was that? That was **Brahma**, Lord Vishnu's servant. Lord Vishnu commanded Brahma, "It is time to begin! Create the world!"

But, before Brahma could begin to create the world, suddenly two **demons** *Madhu* and *Kaitabbha*, sprang forth to kill Brahma. Startled, Brahma prayed hard to Vishnu for protection. Vishnu fumed and frowned at the demons. From his frown, emerged **Lord SHIV** holding a trident! With his trident, Shiv destroyed the demons!

Lord Shiv killing the Demons

The Trinity of Gods and the Hindu Philosophy ...

Brahma, the Creator

Vishnu, the Preserver

Shiv, the Destroyer

The four heads of Brahma show that he has knowledge of all things. His vehicle is a swan.

Vishnu comes to restore order and peace to the world. Vishnu carries a conch shell, a club and a discus or chakra. The chakra is a magic weapon which he hurls at evil enemies

Shiv rules over the death and life of everything in the world. In the centre of his head is a powerful 'third eye'. If he opens it, it will destroy everything in its path.

BRAHMA-VISHNU-SHIV is called the trinity of Gods. They represent the rules of nature that the life cycle follows. The rules are:

1) Everything has to be created. **2)** It needs to be protected. **3)** Eventually, what is created is destroyed, to bring in the new! Thus, if Shiv destroys, it is only to make way for new things. Here is one example, like the day is created as morning, is protected into noon and dusk and later destroyed into night, to be born again the next morning! Therefore, creation-protection-destruction is an endless life cycle.

So, *Brahma* continued his formation. Winds swept up and the waters churned. Brahma raised his hands and calmed them down. *Brahma* then split the lotus flower into three parts. With the first part he created the heavens, the second part the earth and the third part he made the skies. He filled the earth with the energy of life. He made flowers, grass, plants, trees, animals, birds, insects, fishes and many more things. To all this, he gave the ability to see, touch, hear, smell and move. Brahma also fashioned countless stars, heavens and planets.

Some of the other Gods...

Brahma appointed Gods called *'Devas'* to manage the heavenly kingdoms.

God **Indra** is the chief administrator of the heavens! He used thunderbolts to kill the demons or storm clouds to release rains on the earth! Indra rode a white elephant called *Airaawat*! The seven-coloured rainbow is his bow and pour of rain are his arrows!

Even though, Indra has so many weapons he is a peaceful, heavenly ruler who is very kind, generous and helpful. The other Gods caring for the celestial empires are: **Vayu**, *the god of the wind*, **Varun**, the God of rains and **Som**, the moon God! And many, many more!

Among these is **Surya,** the great Sun- god. Surya is shown as a red man with three eyes and four arms, riding in a chariot drawn by seven mares. **Agni**, is the *fire god*. It is said anything touched by him becomes pure.

Indra, the rain God

Surya, the Sun God

Some Gods also have more than one name. For example, *Shiv* is also known as *Shankar, Mahadev, Mahesh or Natraj* (the Lord of Dance). Shiv's dancing symbolizes the eternal energy that flows through the world. It causes the pattern of day and night, the changing of the seasons and the cycle of birth and death.

Shiv's dance of destruction and creation

Kalki

Vamana

Ram

Buddha

Parshuram

Narsingha

Krishna

Varaha

Incarnations of God...

It is believed that whenever there is turmoil and the world is in peril, God incarnates or comes to earth in various forms to restore order and peace. God Vishnu incarnated **ten times.** Each time he appeared in a different form. We shall read about some of these incarnations later in the book.

Matsya

Kurma

The ten Avtars
of Vishnu

Vishnu appeared as **Matsya** (fish), **Kurma** (tortoise), **Varaha** (boar), **Narsingha** (man-lion), **Vamana** (dwarf), **Parashuram** (Ram with Axe), **Ram**, **Krishna**, **Buddha** and **Kalki**.

The Devas and the Asuras...

Over time some Gods became greedy and evil and turned into demons or 'Asuras'. They began to live in the lower heavenly kingdom! Asuras kept fighting and troubling the Devas for their territory in the heavens!

The Asuras

The Gods' Wives or the Goddesses...

Lakshmi,
the Goddess of wealth

The Trinity and the other Gods have their own consorts or wives also. The wives of the Gods worked side by side with their husbands to fight for peace in the heavens. They are worshipped as Goddesses in their own rights too! The Goddesses are mostly called 'Ma' meaning mother.

Vishnu's wife is **Laxmi** the Goddess of wealth. She is shown seated on a lotus flower. Brahma's wife is **Saraswati,** the Goddess of education, wisdom and learning. Her vehicle is a swan and she carries a *vina* (musical instrument) and a book.

Parvati,
the Goddess of peace

Saraswati,
the Goddess of education

Shiv's spouse is **Parvati,** the Goddess of Peace. At times, she can be beautiful and gentle. At other times she takes the form of the warrior goddess, **Durga**.

Durga rides on the back of a lion and slays the evil buffalo demon, *Mahisha*. Sometimes she is Goddess **Kali**, all-powerfull and terrifying, wearing a garland of human skulls, the bringer of disease, strife and war.

Goddess **Kali** was created to defeat the demons *Chandra* and *Mundra*. *Kali* is considered the female version of *Shiv* as a destroyer too.

Kali, the female
version of Shiv

Durga killing demon Mahisha

The 'Amrit' or the Nectar of Immortality...

The *Asuras* and the *Devas* were bitter enemies and the relationship between them pretty grim. But, there is an instance when the *Asuras* and the *Devas* got together!

This is when they churned the ocean of milk to get to the nectar or **'Amrit'** of life which lay deep down! By drinking this nectar, one would never die and become immortal! The *Asuras* and the *Devas* planned to churn the ocean to bring up the nectar.

God Vishnu as Kurma, the tortoise

Have you seen how your grandma churned butter-milk or lassi in a pot? Similarly, to churn the ocean a rod and a rope were needed. The *Devas* and the *Asuras* met at mountain Meru, the abode of the Gods at the centre of the world, to discuss how to churn the ocean. They decided to transfer the **mountain Mandara** into the middle of the ocean and use it as a rod! A very tough task indeed! **Garuda,** the eagle like bird deity, carried Mandara on his back and placed it into the middle of the milky ocean. What would they use as a rope? The **serpent Vasuki** was used as a rope! The *Devas* picked up Vasuki's head but the *Asuras* rudely snatched it out of their hands.

"Why should we be at the tail-end of things?" the *Asuras* shouted. "We will hold the head." The *Devas* readily agreed and lined up gripping the tail firmly.

The Devas and the Asuras churning the ocean

The *Devas* pulled one side and the *Asuras* the other side and churned! But, as they began to churn the ocean, the great mountain started to sink, making it impossible to churn. The mountain had no solid support beneath it. Vishnu then changed himself into a tortoise, **Kurma** and dived underneath to balance the mountain on his back! For a thousand years, the *Devas* and the *Asuras* churned the ocean but nothing emerged from it. Vasuki became angry after being tugged and pulled for so long. Burning hot vapours of venom came out of his nose, scorching the *Asuras* who now wished they had the tail-end; but it was too late.

As Vasuki's anger mounted, great streams of poison gushed out of his mouth! Shiv saved everyone by immediately consuming the poison!

Vishnu as Mohini
distracting the Asuras

His fair, strong neck turned blue as the poison slid down his throat. Thereafter, Shiv came to be known as 'Neel Kanth' or the one with the blue neck.

The Devas and the Asuras resumed their churning and after a while things began to emerge! First came the divine cow, then the divine horse and the elephant, followed by the wish fulfilling-tree and many more treasures! But, it was the final treasure they were after and that was the Amrit or the nectar of immortality! At last, the great healer **Dhanvantari** emerged, carrying the jar of Amrit in his arms. The Asuras snatched the jar from him, refusing to give any nectar to the Devas.

"Vishnu, help us!" the Devas cried out. "If the Asuras drink the Amrit, they would become immortal and would never be defeated!" Then, Vishnu changed himself into a comely maiden called **Mohini**. Her ravishing beauty distracted the Asuras whilst the Devas drank up all the Amrit, leaving none for the Asuras! Later on, this entire exercise of churning the ocean for the treasure of immortality was said to be what a human's life would eventually mean. Man would 'churn' through many stages of chaotic existence to break the endless life cycle and reach the treasure of never ending peace or 'Moksha'!

The Creation of Man on Earth

How did 'Man' grace the lands of earth? Legends say that after Saraswati and Brahma got married, they had a son called **Manu**. Manu was sent to earth as the first human! Manu got married to **Ananti** and they started the human race which you and I are a part of! Subsequent to putting humans on earth, Brahma then decided everyone's fate for a trillion years! Yes, fate or destiny of each human is supposed to have been already decided! That is why the phrase, "What has to happen will happen", is often repeated! You know what Brahma's age is today? *155.521972 trillion years!*

It is said at the end of Brahma's life, the Universe shall end and be recreated all over again!

The start of the human race

Rishis and Saadhus concentrating to gain knowledge about creation

How do we know all this? Fables state that Lord Vishnu breathed the truth to Brahma about the reality of existence. Brahma in turn told his celestial companions, who carried the stories to the first souls on earth who were the *Rishis* and *Sadhus* (saints). The first souls on earth would sit under trees or at the edges of the seas or peaks of the mountains. They would concentrate towards wanting to gain the truth and knowledge about the confusing reasons of why they were on earth.

The Vedas and the Origin of Hinduism

What are the *Vedas*? The *Vedas* are the holy books of Hinduism and perhaps the oldest books in the world. They are four in number - the **Rigveda**, the **Yajurveda**, the **Samaveda** and the **Atharvaveda**. Who wrote these books? These were not written down with ink and paper. It is believed the Vedas were directly revealed from the heavens to the *rishis* and saints on earth. Can you imagine, the revelations or telling of the holy Vedas were uncovered to the saints orally! The *rishis* grasped the Veda revelation through the vibrations of *Mantras*.

*Passing on of Vedas
through speech*

The saints or the *rishis* memorized them and passed them on to further generations! Not a single word was written and the Vedas had to be learnt by heart. These unwritten Vedas are called as **'Shruti'** scriptures. 'Shruti' means 'heard', 'experienced' and 'spiritually revealed'.

The written Vedas or 'Smriti' scriptures

Later, the Vedas were compiled and put on paper. They were written in the **Sanskrit** language. The written Vedas are called **'Smriti'** scriptures. 'Smriti' scriptures include the two great Hindu epics of **'Ramayan'** and **'Mahabharat'**. As years went by, there were many additions to the Vedas. The Vedas form the basis of the faith we call Hinduism!

What do the Vedas Say?...

The Vedas proclaim that all beings are made up of five elements - **Earth (Prithvi)**, **Water (Apaha)**, **Fire (Tejas)**, **Air (Vayu)**, **Ether or atmosphere (Akaasa)**. This means that we have nature inside us as well as outside us!

Rishis, by their concentrated prayer, saw the existence of the ONE Supreme Being or GOD and the five elements we call nature. Even though there are so many Gods and Goddesses, there is only **ONE SUPREME GOD**!

The revelations were in the forms of hymns and were divided into four main parts. The *Rig Veda*, supposedly the oldest and the most holy of the scriptures in the world, contains praise of the Gods. The *Yajur Veda*, includes '**Mantras**' recited at various important occasions. *Sama Veda* contains the knowledge of science and music. *Atharva Veda* is a collection of rituals performed at specific occasions.

The **Upanishads** form a part of the Vedas. The Upanishads are philosophical inquiries or exploring of knowledge, asking about the purpose of life, origin of the world time and space. The **Puranas** were composed for the use of the average Hindu. It contains complex ideas and truths from the Vedas and the Upanishads and explains them in the form of simple stories.

Hinduism, the World's Oldest Living Faith

It is difficult to pinpoint when Hinduism started or who should be given credit for its creation. It has no central figure, such as Christ in Christianity, Muhammad in Islam or the Buddha in Buddhism. Instead it offers the teachings of many great religious thinkers who lived at different times. There is no single sacred book but many different books dating from various times and places. Hinduism is not the result of a single age, but a religion that grew up gradually, collecting together the beliefs of many groups of people.

One God or 330 million Gods...

How many gods and goddesses does Hinduism have? The figure 330 million is sometimes quoted, so is the figure one. And strange as it may seem, both are right. Hinduism recognizes that many people need a god they can feel close to, a god they can picture in their minds and worship.

The various gods and goddesses are various facets of the Supreme Being. For a Hindu, God is ONE, we may call him by any name. We pray to the representations of God, which has taken the shape of either a human, an animal or even trees and rivers. It is said to get better understanding or comprehension, we humans have given God many forms! All these Gods and Goddesses resemble humans, animals or natural forces such as wind, water, fire, sun, and moon; each has different powers to bless the world!

Hindus praying to various representations of God

The Aryans

The Origin of the Word 'Hinduism'...

How did this faith get the name 'Hinduism'? As you know, the Vedas were initially only spoken and nothing was written down till much later! No one was sure of its origin! Some believe that the **Aryans,** who came to India as nomadic tribes, moving from place to place with herds of cattle settled along the river **Indus**. The river Indus was actually the ancient river *Sindhu*. Since *'Sindhu'* was pronounced as *'Hindu'*; this land was called **Hindustan**, the people, **Hindus** and their faith, **Hinduism**! On the other hand, *Sadhus* and *Rishis* insist that Hinduism has directly been communicated from the heavens and is as old as the earth! Over the years, they have carried this message to one and all and the faith of Hinduism has spread far and wide! Today, Hinduism is the third largest religion in the world.

The Teachings of Hinduism

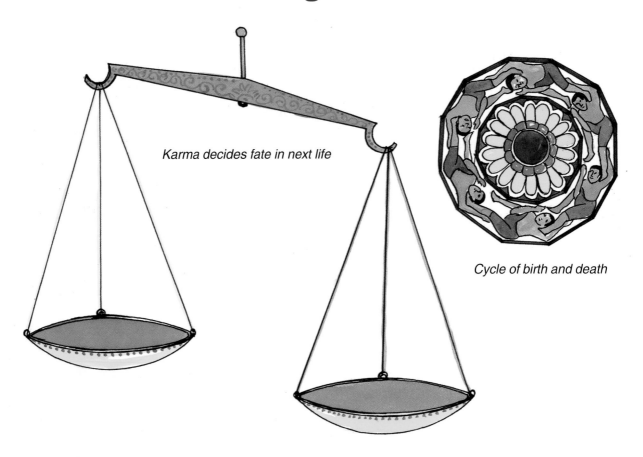

Karma decides fate in next life

Cycle of birth and death

The Cycle of Birth and Death...

Hinduism believes in the cycle of birth and death. It says the soul inside us never dies and is born again and again. According to our scriptures or writings in the holy books, a soul passes into a body at birth and transfers into another body at death. This is called re-incarnation. It is like when we change old clothes for new! But, what kind of new body will the soul journey to? The scriptures say that all this depends on the deeds or **Karma** done in the old body and soul! It depends on your Karma whether you take birth as a human or any other living being. Good karma in the present life leads to an excellent next life and bad karma in the present life leads to a terrible next life. This cycle continues till you find freedom from it and gain release or '**Moksha**' *never to be born again* and live with God forever!

Paths to be one with God...

Hinduism believes in living life according to **DHARMA**. By following Dharma, you could reach God by yourself. What is Dharma? *Dharma* is **following the correct behaviour** in life. Dharma should be a way of life. Prayer, acceptance, tolerance, respect for elders, kindness to fellow human beings and living creatures, deep gratefulness to the divine - is the Dharma everyone should follow.

Correct behaviour or Dharma

River & Animal Deities

Ganga falling on Shiv's head before coming to earth

Hinduism says that God resides everywhere. Trees, rivers and animals are to be worshipped too!

THE STORY OF RIVER GANGA

There is a story about how the holy river **GANGA** came to earth from heaven. Since her force was so strong that if she fell directly onto earth, it would split into two; Shiv offered to take the first impact on his *own head* before the *Ganga* flowed down on earth!

If a Hindu takes a dip in the Ganga river, it is believed that all his or her sins will be washed away!

Most Hindus try to bathe in the river at least once in their lifetime. At the ancient city of **Benares**, the shores of the river are crowded with pilgrims who come to bathe in its holy waters. As the Hindus cremate the body after death (they do not bury it); they have their ashes scattered in the river Ganga or Ganges. Relatives carry the dead person's ashes from distant parts of India or the world to the holy river.

Hindus taking a dip in the holy Ganga river

THE STORY OF GANESH

GANESH, also known as Ganapati, is the *elephant- headed* Hindu God. He is the *son of Shiv and Parvati*. The story of the birth of Ganesh goes like this: Myth has it that Parvati created a beautiful boy from the dirt of her body, treated him as her son and gave him the responsibility of guarding her home.

Shiv and Ganesh

Shiv, her husband, did not know about this. When he returned home, he was surprised to find a young boy standing outside his home. The boy refused to let Shiv into his own home! Shiv became angry and a clash ensued. The fall out was that Shiv chopped the boy's head off!

On discovering this, Parvati was plunged into gloom and deep grief. Contrite Shiv, then sent his soldiers to bring the head of the first being they see sleeping facing north, from the forest. The soldiers came across an elephant.

Thus, an elephant head was brought and placed on the life less boy. With his new elephant head, the boy came alive and he became Ganesh, the one with the elephant head !

However, his mother Parvati still simpering at Shiv's mistake asked for more favours for her son. She asked her husband Shiv to grant Ganesh the title of the **God of Wisdom** as well as **remover of obstacles**. His name should be invoked before entering heavens or before any ceremonies. Also whoever worshipped Ganesh, would be richer with success and property! "So be it!" said Shiv. Along with Brahma and Vishnu all favours amongst many others were granted! Ganesh was made the leader of Shiv's *ganas* (assistants) and thus became **Ganapati**.

Ganesh is regarded by one and all as the **remover of obstacles** and should be **worshipped first**, before any form of worship is offered to any other God. He is also the **Lord of Grammarians**. Many books printed in India have a small picture of him on the title page or the phrase '*Shri Ganesha Namah*' *(reverence to Lord Ganesh).*

Ganesh becomes Ganpati

The story of Ram and Ravan

This story forms one of the most popular Indian epics called Ramayan. It was written in Sanskrit by sage Valmiki. This is included in the 'Smriti' scriptures.

Many thousand years ago, as the *Sadhus* and *Rishis* prayed and meditated, wicked demons or *Rakshasas*, troubled them! Who were *Rakshasas*? *Rakshasas* were suspected to be fallen angels. They were beings that had prayed so hard to the Gods that they had got boons, which made them very, very powerful! What are boons? Boons are favours from the Gods which can make anyone invincible. They had the power to even take the form of animals! The *Rishis* were distraught. They prayed to the Gods begging for protection.

Rakshasa
troubling
Saadhus

God Vishnu's born or re-incarnated as Ram

The Gods in heaven went to Vishnu asking for protection from a particular evil *Rakshas* called **Ravan**. Ravan lived on earth and was very powerful. Vishnu promised the Gods that he, himself, would assume the human form and come to earth to help them. He said he would be born as **Ram**, the son of *King Dashrath of Ayodhya*. True enough, a son was born to King Dashrath. He was called Ram. Ram was the finest example of goodness. Many years later, when Ram was the young Prince of Ayodhya, he was banished into the forest for fourteen years. His stepmother, Kaikeyi, did not want him but her son and Ram's step- brother, Bharat, to ascend the throne. Thus, she used a boon granted by King Dashrath to get rid of Ram. Prince Ram, his wife Sita and brother Laxman went into the forest to live out the fourteen year term.

One day, Sita saw a beautiful golden deer in front of their hut in the forest. She tried to pet it, but it moved away. Sita, of course, did not know that the deer was actually Ravan's soldier who had changed form! Sita begged Ram to chase the deer and get it for her! Ram ran after the deer but could not catch him. Running out of patience, he struck it with an arrow. The fallen deer imitated Ram's voice calling out to Laxman for help. Hearing the voice, Sita panicked and sent Laxman to look for her husband. Ravan was waiting for this opportunity. He tricked Sita into stepping out of the hut and kidnapped her!

Why would he do that? Well, a few days ago, Laxman had insulted his (Ravan's) sister and cut off her nose. Secondly, he found Sita to be very beautiful! Sita was abducted by Ravan and carried off to his kingdom of Lanka across the seas! Ram gathered an army to rescue Sita. But in the forest, there are no warriors, are there? So, his army consisted of bears and monkeys. The most famous monkey was Hanuman.

Hanuman, the Monkey God

He is considered to be a God now. Why is he considered to be God? Besides being totally devoted to Ram, Hanuman was also brave, just and had magical powers which enabled him to fly. In homage to Hanuman, monkeys are rarely harmed in India.

With this Army, Ram went to Lanka, defeated Ravan and brought peace to the forests! It is said that every age will see God in human form, descending to the earth to vanquish evil!

Ram kills Ravan

Krishna

Furthermore, came another saga where God in the form of a human, descended on earth to banish evil. That was the time when the evil Kauravs ruled the place and they unfairly banished their five Pandav cousin brothers into the forest. Here again a war ensued. This war was completely unfair because the five Pandav brothers were pitted against hundred Kaurav brothers. God came to the help of Pandavs in the form of Krishna. Through sane advice and call for duty, Krishna guided the Pandavs through the war, which is called the **Mahabharat**. **Mahabharat** is the second epic written. It is also a smriti scripture and was written by sage **Vyas**.

Tales say Krishna as a child, was very naughty. Krishna was born to Devaki but adopted by Yashoda under peculiar circumstances. But that is another story. One day, his mother Yashoda asked him if he had eaten dirt. Krishna refused so she asked him to open his mouth. Little Krishna did just that and you know what Yashoda saw? Yashoda saw the entire Universe in her son's mouth! She saw the sun, the moon, the earth, the stars, pinpoints in the void. As she saw them, she was aware that she herself, was an insignificant speck, standing on a tiny planet staring into her son's mouth! That is when she realized her adopted son was someone special!

Yashoda sees the entire universe in Krishna's mouth

The Bhagvad Gita

Lord Krishna's discourse on duty was written as the **Bhagvad Gita** and is considered a holy book even now! The Bhagvad Gita is contained in the Mahabharat. As said, the cousins Pandavs and Kauravs were involved in a fight in the battle of Kurukshetra. Krishna, who possessed a godly power and who was a relative of the family, took the side of Pandavs. During the battle, Krishna worked as a charioteer for **Arjun**, one of the Pandav brothers and Krishna's disciple. Suddenly, Arjun refused to fight at this battle-field. When he looked at the other side he did not see enemies, but his own brothers! He was overcome with emotion and could not recognize his call for duty. It is here that Lord Krishna preached the Bhagvad-Gita to Arjun! Krishna spoke of all the reasons why Arjun should fight. During the discourse, Krishna revealed himself as the *avatar* or manifestation of Lord Vishnu to the astonished Arjun. Krishna took on his shape as the universal one or **'Vishwa Roop'**! Showing this multi dimensional form, Krishna persuaded Arjun to fight.

Krishna shows his 'Vishwa Roop' form to Arjun

What did Krishna say?...

Krishna spoke of all the reasons why Arjun should fight! Krishna told Arjun that the most important thing is to do one's duty without worrying about the results. Krishna said, "Do not grieve for the loss of bodies because body is mortal and soul is immortal." What does this mean? It means that our cycle of life continues even after death in the form of soul. The life we get in the next birth depends on our deeds or *Karma*.

The Bhagvad Gita

Krishna said, "Remember Arjun, it is not who you fight that is important, but what you fight for." Regardless of victory or defeat, pleasure or pain, as a *Kshatriya* (warrior), he, Arjun, had a duty to wage this righteous war! Krishna spoke about the necessity to focus on performing one's proper duty while keeping the body and mind sound and calm.

Krishna's words of wisdom managed to clear the confusion in Arjun's mind and prepared him to fight the battle. Arjun fought like a true hero and the pandavs emerged victorious. The battle of Kurukshetra marked the victory of Truth and Justice. All the teachings of Krishna are contained in the Bhagvad Gita which is a very sacred book of the Hindus. The Bhagvad Gita is highly respected among the sacred writings of the world and has been translated into numerous languages.

Similarity between historical weapons & modern day weapons

The Weapons of War, Similar to Modern Day Weapons...

This is one of the unique features described in the holy books. Whilst reading about the weapons used in these wars, a comparison with modern day weapons automatically comes to the mind! The weapons of those times were largely **bows and arrows**! But, the arrows were more like **modern missiles** than simple arrows. These arrows were fit to carry explosives with destructive power similar to modern day **atom bombs**! Other arrows could be zeroed on to exact targets! There were even arrows capable of deactivating other arrows, similar to modern day **anti-missiles**. There were also **flying birds and animals** with characteristics and features very similar to the present day **aeroplanes**! Wow! This sounds fantastic, does it not? Especially, because these books were written several hundred years ago!

The Caste System

Society's division according to man's body parts

As the earth grew, the population of humans did too. Rishis' said that when God created man, he also provided a division of his society according to man's body parts. His mouth was a **Brahmin**, who would be educator and tell the people about God. The arms of man were warrior princes or **Kshatriyas** who would fight and protect everyone. His thighs, were the one who plies trade or were the **Vaishyas**. Some beliefs also claim the Vaishyas being the stomach! Finally, the feet were the labour or **Shudras**!

According to these instructions, each divided section of the ancient culture used their natural talents to make a strong and growing society for the populace!

However, as time passed, the educated section became so arrogant that they passed a rule that no one could switch occupations! They said once born into a caste they had to remain so all their lives! Higher caste, middle caste and lower caste, divided society.

The upper caste exploited the lower caste. The lower castes were considered menial workers and untouchables! The caste system was so rigid that people belonging to different castes could not marry each other. How horrid! This division of society was very shameful as this promoted the belief that some humans were better than the others. But, God never intended this.

Brahmin exploiting the Shudra or labour class

Ram and Lakshman with Shabri

The story of Shabri...

There is this beautiful story about an old lady called **Shabri**. She was considered to be low caste. One day, Prince Ram of Ayodhya, who is supposed to be the **re-incarnation of Lord Vishnu**, came to her village in search of Sita. Shabri was very excited on seeing him and wanted to greet Ram with berries freshly picked from the forest. "They have to be sweet," she told herself. Sitting before him, she bit each berry, offering him only the sweet ones!

The villagers were aghast and could not think of the high caste Prince eating the already bitten berries by the low caste Shabri! But, Ram courteously accepted Shabri's loving offering without even once frowning or refusing. He ate with great satisfaction.

So, what do we learn from this story? That actually God does not believe in untouchables and castes and all are equal in his eyes! The priests had started controlling the entire society claiming that they were the direct link to God. Meaningless rituals and unreasonable superstitions popped up! That surely was not what the Hindu Vedas had predicted, I am sure! The true meaning of Hinduism is not about dividing society or ignoring one's basic duty of helping mankind. That is why the theory of reincarnation is believed in. Be good, do your duty and keep faith. If you have sinned, you will have to pay for it; not only in this birth but in rebirth too! Life is about kindness, understanding, harmony and fairness. That is why throughout decades, God in some form or the other is said to have descended on earth to banish the demons of greed, unfairness and cruelty!

Brahmin fooling the man to follow mindless superstitions

Shirdi Sai Baba...

Sai Baba was considered to be one of the greatest saints of the 20th century. In fact, he was first seen as a youth of sixteen sitting under a neem tree in Shirdi. No one knew where he came from or what religion he belonged to. He was just there. His peaceful and calm personality attracted many and so did his messages. He seemed to have a wealth of knowledge!

He said he had come to serve mankind and free them from the clutches of fear. What fear? All those fears which trouble living beings. Sai Baba said he was also here to remind them that God was there to help them. Sai Baba showed no desires for worldly possessions and maintained a completely simple way of life.

He remained within the society of the poor and was always solving their problems. He preached the fact that people should not highlight personal problems and always remember God. He wanted to revive a wish for the spiritual life as well as faith in humanity. For Sai Baba, all religions were the same. He treated everyone alike.

Soon people also realized that this Baba who had suddenly come to live with them was no ordinary individual but a person with remarkable Godly powers.

Shirdi Sai Baba

As time passed, everyone began to believe him to be an *avtaar* or an incarnation of God. For Sai Baba, praying in temples or Mosques was the same thing.

Did you know that the Hindus considered Sai Baba as Guru and God both; the Muslims regarded Baba as a Guru (Saint) proving that caste, community or creed do not matter to God. When this youth came and settled in Shirdi he began to perform miracles and actually displayed a healing touch. Stories of blind people getting their sight back as well as curing of diseases by his touch were heard.

Then, there is the story of burning lamps (diyas) with water instead of oil! Yes, Sai Baba would daily take oil from a grocer to light lamps in the mosque and temples. One day, the grocer lied as he felt he did not want to give free oil to Sai Baba. The grocer made up a story saying he did not have fresh stocks! That day, Baba returned home without oil. Then, he went to the mosques and temples and poured water instead of oil into the lamps. He actually lit the wicks of the lamps with water instead of oil! The lamps burned till midnight! On seeing this, the Grocer was awed at first and then repented his action. He asked for Sai Baba's forgiveness.

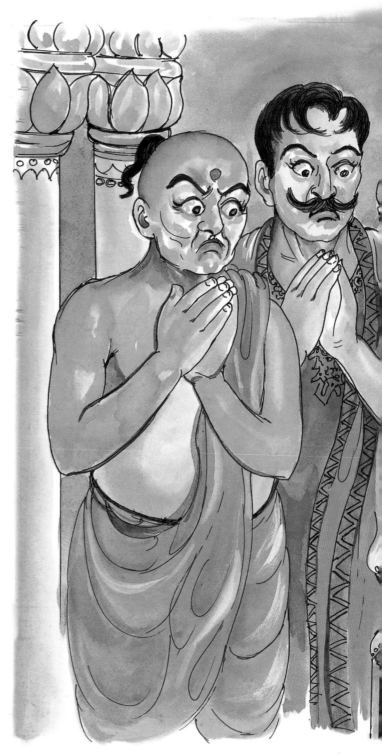

Sai Baba said, "You should have refused to give me oil, but you did not have to lie that you didn't have fresh stocks?" Of course, Sai Baba forgave the grocer but not before extracting a promise from him to never lie ever again!

Sai Baba attracted devotees from all over the country though he never travelled and never cared for fame.

Sai Baba lighting the diyas with water

Sai Baba left this earth on **15th October, 1918** leaving behind a message of tolerance, universal brotherhood, love, simple living and to rise above negativity like ego and selfishness. Sai Baba was buried in Shirdi and a beautiful shrine has been built there. To this day, people flock to Shirdi to pay homage to Sai Baba.

The Hindu Family System

The undivided Hindu Family

Hindus have very strong family bonds. Do you know what that means? In Hinduism, a man or a woman does not lead individual lives but life of his or her family! It is believed that family bond carries on through existence and we are all in some way or the other, related from our past lives!

A son of the family must look after his aged parents. This is a good system because when you grow old and cannot look after yourself, it is good to have someone young to make things comfortable! The Hindu joint family is the foundation of the Hindu traditional society. Blood relations are close and one. That means brothers, sisters, uncles, aunts, nieces, nephews, all related by blood, are one big family!

Respect for the elders and care for the youngsters is a value, which goes with family relationships always! The family is founded on the belief of DHARMA. Hindus are very possessive about their children and spend a great deal of their time and energy in bringing them up. The bond between the parents and children remains intact even after the children grow up and become independent!

A son of the Hindu family is expected to carry ahead the family line and the family name with respect and pride. However, things are slowly changing nowadays! Sadly, old people are increasingly suffering from problems of isolation, indifference and neglect from their own children. Homes for the aged, away from family homes, are now coming up in many parts of India. These were unheard of, a few years ago.

A Story With a Moral Twist...

Once, there was a family of five members ,that is: two aged grandparents, their son, daughter in law and a young grandson. Well, the son and the daughter in law somehow failed to recognize the extra attention their aged parents needed. In fact, they refused to let their son play with his grand parents. Why would they do that? Because they felt that the grand parents were not modern enough! Not only that, they banished the old couple to a shed at the back of their home. One day, the young grandson was playing as his parents sat on the lawns outside their house. Whilst playing, he started collecting twigs and branches. He also questioned his parents about mortar, cement and buildings.

The old grand parents

When his parents asked him why he needed to know, he shrugged and said, "When I grow up and have children, they too will need to be kept away from you; like my grandparents have been kept away from me. So, I was making a shed for you two to stay then!"

The son and the daughter-in-law became shocked when they heard this. Moments later, they realized their mistake and understood the simple truth of life. The little grandson, in a way, explained that life is like a cycle and what goes forward comes back to the same point again! Thus, goes the popular saying, 'As you sow, so shall you reap.' The Hindu Culture also says that elders too should follow the correct rules of behaviour towards their younger ones and build a balance in their interaction with them!

Young grandson asking the parents

So, if the older person is polite to his or her younger friend or family member, then sure enough he or she shall get politeness in return. If you speak rudely, then you too will be meted out rude treatment! Remember this when you speak to anyone regardless of age! This was about the elderly being ignored; however, unfortunately, since a son is preferred in some families, they ill - treat their daughters too! This is something unacceptable, is it not? The joint family system meant generations of family from grand pa and grand ma right till the youngest of grandchild lived beneath one roof! Time sees more and more families breaking away from this system.

Many feel that the change from traditional joint family system has brought on many problems that include loneliness, stress and depression.

The Four Stages of Hindu Life...

Hinduism acknowledges four main stages of life. These are **student**, **householder**, **retired** person and **sanyasi** or the Hindu holy man. A sanyasi rejects life and its worldly possessions and roams about, seeking the truth about God and existence. Some Hindus, but not many, pass through the four stages but most spend much of their adult lives as householders. Elderly people may adapt to the third stage of retirement and spend much of their time in prayer and meditation while living in a son's home

Student

Householder

Retired person

Sanyasi

How Does a Hindu Pray?

Hindu prayer is an individual prayer where he or she can pray anywhere. Most Hindus see praying as a part of everyday life. However, worship is also done at temples or '**Mandirs**'. God for the Hindus is formless and everywhere; thus, it is necessary to create an image or idol to connect the mind on. *Meditation* or control of senses and mind, is a very popular Hindu practice. Many Hindus pray when they wake up each day and many times during the day. While praying, a Hindu sits facing EAST, where the Mandir of the home should be placed. He/She meditates his or her mind on the images or idols of Gods and Goddesses kept there. The name of the almighty is repeated several times. Many use prayer beads too.

Offerings to Gods include flowers, incense or *'Agarbatti'* and special food for the Gods. It is auspicious to sprinkle around **'Ganga Jal'** or holy water from the holy river Ganges *(Ganga)* to purify the place before prayer. Hindus believe in the power of **'Mantras'**. Mantras sound the name of the divine aloud and purify the air. The most important Hindu Mantra is the **Gayatri Mantra** that admires the presence and virtues of the almighty and shows gratefulness, as well as asks guidance for the right paths towards God.

The Gayatri Mantra:

"We worship that Divine Radiance

May that Divine Radiance illuminate our minds."

When the Hindus pray in groups, the gathering is called a 'Kirtan'. At a Kirtan, hymns or 'Bhajans' are sung collectively in the praise of God. 'Guru' is the teacher who imparts knowledge about true paths to God. In some prayers his name is taken first because in Hinduism it is believed that a Guru has a very high status in society.

Hindu Temples...

A Hindu loves temples and considers it the house of Gods. The temples in India are architectural wonders! Amongst the most famous temples is **Lotus temple in New Delhi**, which is *shaped like a lotus flower!*

Lotus temple

Of the twelve most sacred Shiv temples, **Somnath temple** is one of them. Legends go that it was raided and destroyed six times and rebuilt each time! Mahmud of Ghazni, raided Somnath from his Afghan kingdom and after a two-day-battle, took the town and the temple. Having looted its magnificent wealth, he damaged it quite badly. The priests of the temple begged him to spare the image of Shiv but he smashed it to pieces.

Ghazni destroying Somnath temple

Though the temple was rebuilt again, Somnath always attracted looters for its wealth. So, began a pattern of destruction and rebuilding that continued for centuries! The Somnath temple is located in **Gujarat**. It is believed that the temple is so ancient that it was built by the Moon God himself!

At **Konark** is the beautiful **Sun temple**. This shows Surya or the sun god with 12 pairs of exquisitely carved wheels drawn by galloping horses.

One of the holiest shrines is that of Jagannath temple at **Puri**. In the South, **Meenakshi Temple** is created around a lotus shaped city! **Tirumala** boasts of the wealthiest Vishnu temple.

Somnath temple

The Shrine of **Vaishno Devi** nestled in the hills of **Jammu and Kashmir** draws thousands of worshippers every year in the present day and age!

It is said that the Goddess resides there in a beautiful cave in the form of 3 'Pindis' or rocks namely, **Maha-Kali**, **Maha-Laxmi** and **Maha-Saraswati**.

Shree Dhar, Bhairavnath and Goddess disguised as a girl

The myth of Vaishno Devi says:

About 700 hundred years ago, a humble pundit *(brahmin)* named **Shree Dhar** had a dream. In his dream, a Goddess appeared and asked him to hold a feast for the village and nearby places. The pundit agreed and invited everyone from his village as well as the close by villages. Shree Dhar also invited **Bhairav Nath**, a person who had spiritual powers. Bhairav Nath questioned Shree Dhar on how a poor pundit like him would feed so many people when he had no means to do so. He also warned that if the meal was not up to the standard, the consequences would be terrible for the pundit!

Shree Dhar feared Bhairav Nath and wondered how he, Shree Dhar, would pull off the feast with no money.

"How will I feed so many people? I have no means to do so?" the worried pundit said to himself.

The next moment, the Goddess appeared to him again and said, "Do not worry! Seat over 360 devotees in to the small hut and everything will be alright!" And lo behold, that is exactly what happened! There was good food and everyone ate to full satisfaction. The Goddess also helped Shree Dhar look after the guests. She transformed herself into a girl to do so!

The Goddess kills Bhairav Nath with her trident

Bhairav Nath was amazed at the turn of events and became very curious about this mysterious girl who seemed to have super-natural powers. For nine months, Bhairav Nath was searching for the mystic girl in the mountains. Then one day, he saw the same girl hitting the stone with an arrow and water gushing out of the stone. As he approached her, she suddenly disappeared. Later, he saw her sitting on a mountain peak. But, moments later, again she disappeared. Over there, Bhairav noticed footprints on the stone. Wondering whether she was hiding in the cave, he decided to enter it. On seeing Bhairav entering the cave, the girl with her trident broke a path out of the cave and escaped to another beautiful cave in the mountains!

"Stop! Come no further!"

The girl urged Bhairav not to follow Her. However, he refused to listen to her. When Bhairav entered the cave, the girl took the form of fierce **Chandi**, the *Goddess of Destruction*. With her trident *(trishul)*, she cut Bhairav's head off and killed him! The head of Bhairav fell on the mountain peak. But though his head was separated, he was still conscious. Bhairav repented for his conduct and begged forgiveness. The Goddess accepted his repentance and said that whosoever worshipped Her, would later visit his shrine.

Shrine of Vaishno Devi

But, how did the cave become such a popular shrine? The story says that Shree Dhar kept remembering the cave where he had seen the holy Goddess in his dreams and she had said it was her abode! He went searching for the cave through twisting and turning paths. His only guide was the picture of the cave in his mind, which he had seen in his dreams. At last, he reached the mouth of the cave he had seen in his dreams.

He went in and saw the Goddess in her 'Pindi Rupa' or in the form of three rocks inside the cave. On seeing them, Shree Dhar went into deep reverence, feeling the presence of the Goddess there! The Pundit prayed daily to the Goddess in the cave. Pleased, the Goddess appeared and blessed him saying, "Your future progeny will worship me for a long time to come and they will be blessed with happiness, wealth, health and valour." And from that day on, Shree Dhar's descendants as well as the others spread the word of the Goddess's **'Shakti'**. People traversed hard paths to reach this cave and worship and be blessed by her. This cave is the shrine of Vaishno Devi.

Symbols of Hinduism...

'**Om**' is the most sacred syllable, often chanted during Hindu ceremonies. They are holy letters of the Sanskrit language, the language of God and represent the **Trinity**. The Trinity is composed of the three top Hindu Gods: **Brahma**, *the creator,* **Vishnu**, *the preserver* and **Shiv**, *the destroyer*.

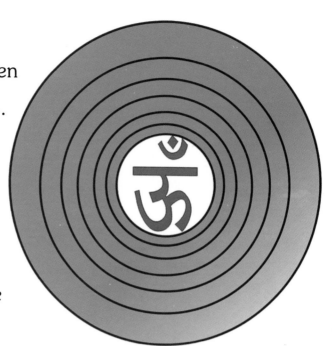

These letters when pronounced properly, creates energy in the mind and body. This sacred syllable is spoken to show God we remember him. This symbol in Hinduism also represents the whole universe.

Another *very important sign* is the '**Swastik**', which is regarded holy by the Hindus. The word swastik means auspicious or lucky in the Sanskrit language. It is used to mean the welcoming of auspiciousness or luck and driving away of evil. The sign also says that nature keeps on changing but God the Supreme-Being is always the same and does not ever change!

Hindu Festivals

The faith of Hinduism completely believes in festivals, which is mostly a celebration of triumph over evil!

Dusshera: A ten-day festival celebrates vanquishing of demons and Ram's victory over Ravan.

Diwali: It is a five- day celebration of lights and crackers to welcome Lord Ram home after his banishment.

Janmashtami: Janmashtami is the birthday celebration of Lord Krishna. At night, songs and stories related to Krishna's birth are sung and narrated. As the moment of Krishna's birth arrives, he is devotionally welcomed. There after sweets are distributed as the mark of joy, since the birth of Krishna denotes the advent of the annihilator of evils.

Ganesh Chaturthi: It is dedicated to Lord Ganesh. Huge processions carrying the images of Ganesh proceed for immersion towards the sea.

Onam: Kerala's harvest festival is celebrated with snake boat races and traditional feasts!

Holika and Prahlad

Holi: A north Indian festival, which symbolizes the destruction of the evil **demon Holika** and also marks the end of winters. Holi, the **festival of colours**, is celebrated in spring on the full moon day! The story behind the festival of holi is:

Once, there was a young boy called **Prahlad**, who believed fully in Lord Vishnu. Sadly, his father, **demon King Hiranyakashyapu**, was totally against this and was very angry at his son's devotion! He tried his level best to divert his son's faith away from Lord Vishnu but was unable to do so! He was extremely angry and decided to kill his son. Hiranyakashyapu commanded his sister Holika to carry Prahlad in her arms and walk into burning flames.

Holika would be saved because she had a boon from the God of flames and the lad in her arms would die. But, exactly the opposite happened. Lord Vishnu saved the lad and Holika died. How did this happen? Hiranyakashyapu did not know that for one hour in the day, the boon or protection from flames did not work.

Narsingha kills Hiranyakashyapu

Unfortunately for Holika, the time chosen to enter the flames and kill the lad fell at the same hour! When the flames leapt up, Holika died as the boon did not work and Prahlad was saved by Lord Vishnu! Later, God Vishnu took the form *(avtaar)* of **Narsingha** *(half man and half lion)* and killed Hiranyakashyapu.

Prahlad was so sorry for Holika that he promised to name a festival after her. So, now we have the festival of Holi. **Lighting of bonfires** an evening before Holi, represents the burning of Holika! Splashing of colours and meeting with family and friends are a part of Holi celebrations!

Raksha Bandhan: When God Indra went to battle, his wife tied a thread charged with sacred protection prayers on his wrist. Through the power of the thread tied on his wrist, it is said that Indra won the battle and defeated his enemies. From this point, the significance of tying a 'protection thread' to near and dear ones, charged with holy verses from the Vedas, started! So, according to these ancient traditions

Indra's wife tying the 'protection' thread

sisters too began to tie a sacred thread on the wrists of their brothers to protect them from all evil. Rakshabandhan is such a day where sisters charge a thread by chanting verses and pray to God for the welfare of their brothers. This thread is called '**Rakhi**'. On this day, a sister can demand a gift from her brother too! When a sister secures a Rakhi on her brother's wrist, her brother too in a way vows to fulfill his brotherly duties at all times! Rakhi is usually a silken rope like thread. But nowadays, Rakhis are becoming more and more fancy.

Rakhi

Philosophers and Thinkers

Swami Vivekanand in America

Swami Vivekanand...

Swami Vivekanand, was one of the many great Indian philosophers and thinkers. He surfaced to fame at the parliament of religions held in **Chicago in 1893**, where he represented Hinduism. Vivekanand's 'Guru' and spiritual master was **Swami Ramakrishna Paramhansa**. He followed his beliefs. Vivekanand asked every one to help mankind and return to the true meaning of Vedas. Why would he do that? Well, during his time, Hinduism was falling into the trap of myths and pointless ceremonies! He believed that the Vedas, if understood properly, were definitely simpler and more sensible.

Vivekanand, like his master, wanted to concentrate on the Almighty and forget the world and its worldly temptations. Yet, his heart went out to the millions in India and the world, who were poor, sick and helpless!

Vivekanand is quoted to have said with great feeling:

"I do not believe in a God or religion which cannot wipe the widow's tears or bring a piece of bread to the orphan's mouth."

This showed compassion and a spirit of nationalism too! Vivekanand wanted to use religion as a method to help and uplift people who were suffering from poverty and sickness. Not as a way to threaten and overpower people with superstitions and meaningless rituals. Vivekanand had a triumphant address at America! Up till then, the Americans thought that Indians were superstitious and ignorant. Thanks to him, India was honoured not only in America but in the entire world too. To help the masses through an organized effort, he started **Sri Ramakrishna Mission** in 1897.

Maha Rishi Dayanand Saraswati...

*Maha Rishi
Dayanand Saraswati*

Dayanand Saraswati founded the **'Arya Samaj'** in 1875 at Mumbai. It is claimed that the Arya Samaj is not a "religion but an organization". It was formed to veer a Hindu society, which was becoming steeped in rituals, superstitions, untouchability and prayers to too many Gods, back to the Vedic system and principles.

Contribution of Hinduism to the World

Navagrahas or Hindu Astronomy...

The science of Astronomy has been referred to in the Vedas, long before famous astronomers were even born! The Hindu sages spoke of knowledge about the universe and the planets. It is an accepted fact that the Hindus were he original **masters of astronomy** through which they discovered **astrology**. They said that astrology or foretelling of the future depended largely on the position of the planets and their movements.

Astrologer studying position of planets

Praying to all the nine grahas (planets), which are:

1. **Surya** (Sun)
2. **Chandra** (Moon)
3. **Mangal** (Mars)
4. **Budh** (Mercury)
5. **Brihaspathi** (Jupiter)
6. **Sukra** (Venus)
7. **Sani** (Saturn)
8. **Rahu**
9. **Ketu**

gives us serenity or peace and remove problems from our way. The names of the seven bodies (Sun, Moon, Mars, Mercury, Jupiter, Venus, Saturn) are still connected, in some languages, with the seven days of the week. All astrology is totally based on the planetary movements and its effect on human beings. Hindus believe that the fate of humans is decided well in advance by the placement of the nine planets. The nine planets are collectively known as 'Navagrahas'.

Vishnu cuts off
Rahu's head

THE STORY OF RAHU AND KETU

Remember the story about the churning of the ocean? Well, there is more to the story. As you know, the nectar of life or the *Amrit* was only to be drunk by the Devas and the *Asuras* had to be distracted. When Vishnu was distracting the Asuras by changing into a maiden called Mohini, one *Asura* realized this and changed himself into a *Deva* (god) to drink the *Amrit*. But, as the *Asura* was about to have the nectar; **Surya**, the Sun God and **Chandra**, the Moon God, cried out,

"Stop! That's Rahu, the *Asura*!"

The next moment, Vishnu disguised as Mohini, revealed himself and his divine weapon, the *chakra*, appeared in his hands.

Before the Nectar could pass through Rahu's throat, the chakra cut off his head. But some drops of the nectar had been swallowed by the demon. Therefore, his body and severed head became immortal or undying. The head of the *Asura* is called '**Rahu**' and his torso '**Ketu**'.

It is believed that this immortal head and body occasionally swallow the sun or the moon, **causing eclipses**. Then, the sun or the moon pass through the opening at the neck, ending the eclipse. Why does Rahu and Ketu swallow the moon or the sun? Because the sun and the moon were the ones who pointed out to Vishnu that Rahu was an *Asura* in disguise.

Immortal Rahu swallowing the sun causing eclipse

Yoga, Ayurveda and Yagnas...

Hindu Sages and Sadhus, applied intense yoga and reached unbelievable physical and mental heights! Many of us think Yoga is some form of work- out or gym exercise! Actually, Yoga comes from the Sanskrit verb 'yuj' which means to 'yoke' or 'unite'. Yoga promotes health. It improves efficiency of joints, nerves, glands, internal organs and spine through steady and various poses or **asanas**. The **asanas** start up the seven energy centres in the human body called **Chakras**. This will give you good health and better concentration on God. It also teaches **breath control** and **mental agility**. Yoga is so popular today that people from abroad, travel all the way to India to learn it!

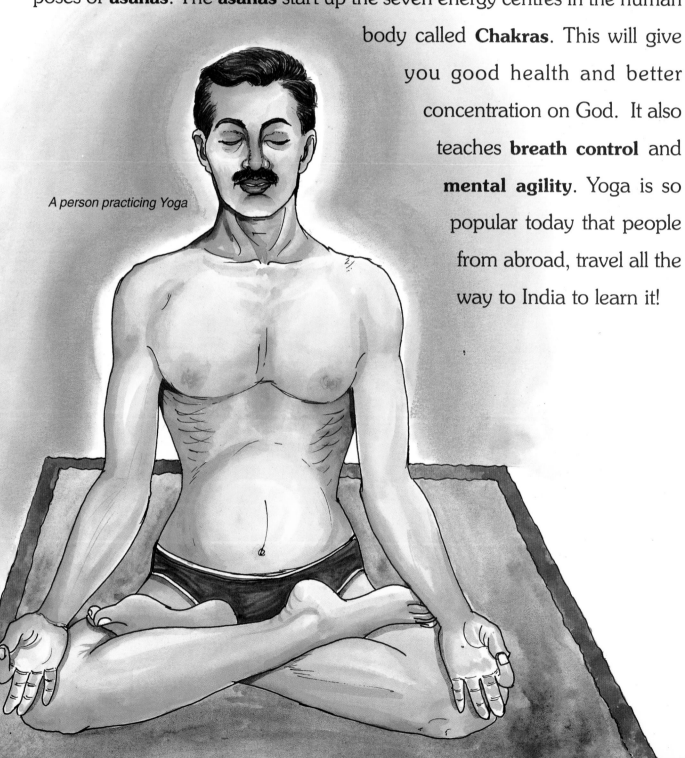

A person practicing Yoga

The Vedas believe in the performing of **Yagna**, a Hindu practice of prayers and offerings to the highest Gods, through the sacred fire. Hindus believe that *chanting of mantras* and throwing offerings in to the purity of the sacred fire, creates a straight link with the deities or Gods and Goddesses.

Yagna

In Sanskrit, **Ayurveda** means the 'knowledge of life'. Hindu sages and seers, for the well being of humans, gave the Ayurvedic system of healing to mankind more than 5,000 years ago! Medicines made from herbs, plants, even from gold and silver, were used for effective healing treatment. In the modern times, when people are getting aware of the ill-effects of allopathic treatment and medicines, Ayurvedic treatment is becoming increasingly popular throughout the world.

Ayurveda

Most Commonly Asked Questions

Q) What is religion & why is it important?

A) Religion is a system of faith, worship and humans' recognition of personal Gods or God. That means that every section of the cultures worldwide, have a particular system of belief and devotion to their own Gods. This is what is called religion. But, why is it important? Well, it seems when God created the world he put the 'good' and also the 'bad' side by side. 'Bad' meant, evilness, selfishness, might is right, terrorism, criminal actions, cheating, injustice, dishonesty, cruelty, etc. 'Good' prescribed to being fair, just, honest, kind, benevolent, compassionate, helpful, grateful, etc. He also made bad attractive so people were pulled towards it.

Noble actions

Why did he do that? To show people the true test of resisting it (bad) and tracking the suitable ways to create a uniform order in society! This God said came from following the good or the right path! Because if 'bad' was to prevail completely over 'good', there would be terror and chaos and we would live in the law of the jungle! The rule of the bad would mean that the unfair mighty would rule completely over the frightened weak! That would be wrong wouldn't it?

Evil actions

So, religion reveals how to pursue the right conduct! If you ever study all religions, you would notice that each one of them lay down similar rules of behaviour. Hinduism describes dharma as the moral law united with pious regulation that leads one's life. This teaches you codes of life that say be honest, be polite, be just and be grateful to the almighty, who created so much! These codes overcome evil thoughts of temptations, terrorism, unfairness and nastiness, therefore creating a uniform order of behavior. Thus, religion apart from being a form of worship also prescribes rules of correct actions to keep a balance in society. Of course, many misuse religion and misinterpret religious sayings to create unrest in the world and it is for every individual to avoid being influenced by such attempts!

Q) Do the Hindus pray to all the innumerous Gods and Goddesses?

A) No, it is not a rule that a Hindu has to worship all the innumerous Gods and Goddesses! Some Hindus worship only Vishnu. Others worship only Shiv and so on and so forth. Others worship only the Goddesses and call these Goddesses collectively as 'Shakti' meaning strength. Many of these Goddess worshippers worship Parvati in her images as Kali or Durga.

Q) Why can I not see God?

A) Can you 'see' happiness? No, you can only feel happiness! For example, when you get to eat the ice cream of your choice, do you see happiness? Can you touch and hold it? The ice cream is there, but is that happiness? No, happiness is something inside! We can feel a warm spread of some sensation or feeling, which we cannot see. That is what God is. We can feel his presence everywhere.

There is this story about a young student who was asking his teacher again and again why he or anyone could not see God.

"If God is every where, why can't we see him?" was the repeated query by the student!

The teacher answered, "God's presence can be felt and experienced in everything, provided he is first realized in the heart."

The argument went on and the teacher really could not convince the student. In the end, the student losing his patience, said, "If you cannot show me God, then I am leaving."

The student bent low to touch his teacher's feet.

'Thwack'! The teacher gave him his blessings with a hard box on his back. The startled student yelped, feeling the pain acutely.

"It pains, it pains, what have you done?"

The teacher said, "Oh! Does it hurt? Child, show me the pain."

The boy removed his shirt and showed the teacher his bruised back.

The teacher said, "I see the bruise, but where is the pain? Show me the pain."

'Thwack'! Another resounding box.
The youth howled.

"What is the matter with you", the teacher said. "Why are you howling? There is no pain, I don't see anything."

The boy screamed, "What are you saying? How can you see pain? You can't see it, it is invisible, it is inside. You can only feel it. I thought you to be a wise man, can't you understand even this simple truth?"

The teacher laughed on hearing this.

The student looked at him questioningly.

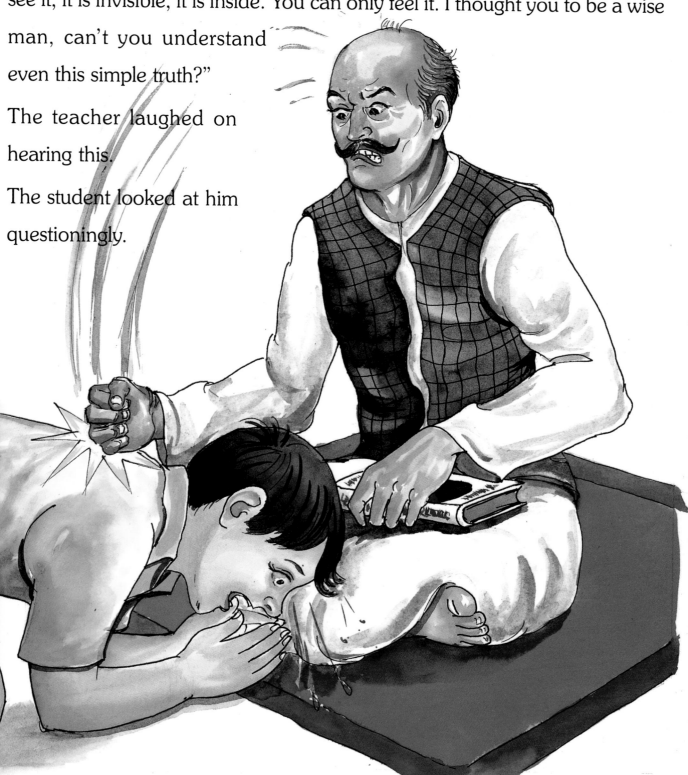

After a few moments, he too laughed. He understood what the teacher had been saying about feeling the presence of God and not being able to 'see' God! The boy thanked the teacher for making him understand.

Q) What is a Hindu marriage all about?

A marriage ceremony, whether it be from the boy's side or the girl's is the most looked forward event in a Hindu family! Traditionally, a Hindu family plays a vital role in bringing the girl and the boy together. What does that mean? That means marriages are mostly arranged by the approval of the family! Actually, Hindu marriages are culturally different in tradition and customs since every region have their own ways of practicing Hinduism. But mostly, the basic rule of taking marriage vows in front of a sacred **fire** prevails and is central to all nuptials. The presence of a **priest** is also vital.

The time-honoured importance of the 'varmala' or exchanging of garlands by the couple is a proposal for marriage made by the bride and the acceptance of the proposal by the groom.

Hindu marriage

It probably originated from the **Swayamvara** practice established in the early centuries in India. The time for the marriage is set by the priest after he has studied the stars and the planets to determine the most auspicious moment. The priest recites hymns from the sacred texts in Sanskrit and the bride and the groom pour small offerings of rice and ghee into the flames.

The most important part of the ceremony comes when a knot is tied between the bride's saree and the groom's *kurta* (long shirt) and the couple walk around the fire together seven times. The seven steps around the fire actually stand for seven wishes. The legend goes that Parvati asked Shiv for seven wishes before marrying him. He agreed to grant the wishes, which roughly asked for faith, togetherness, protection, progeny or children, adjustments and respect for each other.

*Parvati asking for
seven wishes*

In fact, the Hindu marriage is supposed to be an everlasting holy bond between two souls. The boy and the girl promise in front of their family as well as the divine to uphold the sacred vows of marriage.

Marriage also means celebrations and lots of good food and happiness. Both sides of the families make sure the occasion is a memorable one. The Groom or the 'boy' comes like a prince riding a horse amidst song and dance to claim his bride. The bride with all her finery represents not only a princess but also the Goddess Laxmi or the bringer of good luck and happiness. The altar where the rites are performed is called the 'Mandap'. The marriage is the second stage of Hindu life or *Grahastha Ashram* (householder stage)

Unfortunately, marriages and ceremonies today are becoming very complicated and moving away from the simplicity addressed in the Vedas. One of the most serious evils of the Hindu marriages, is the **dowry system**.

This means that the parents of the girl provide the girl with **dowry**. What is dowry? Dowry is giving clothes, furniture, cash, etc., to the girl when she leaves the parent's home to enter her new home or the husband's home.

Sadly, the true meaning has been twisted. Where dowry was a happy present given to the girl starting a new life from her parents, it has now taken on a criminal colour. Now the choice of giving their daughter a simple gift is being taken away by greedy demands! Dowry demands are increasing and being asked for as a right by the groom as well as his parents! A girl is chosen for the dowry she gets and also killed for the dowry she does not get. Even though it is banned, no one seems to care or follow the ban. In fact that is why when a girl is born, some illiterate and even some educated people consider it a curse. The poor parents know that their life savings and peace will be invested into their daughter's marriage and future happiness! But it does not have to be like this because this is not what the system was meant to be! The educated and fair-minded people should raise their voices louder and make sure this system is thrown out and never allowed to return ever again!

Dowry, the social evil

Q) What is the difference between 'OM' and 'Amen'?

A) They both have different meanings. 'OM' is chanted to call the presence of God before any religious ceremony whereas 'AMEN' is pronounced to state belief in the faith at the end of any religious sermons, announcements etc.

Q) What does 'Namaste' mean?

A) Hindus greet each other by bowing the head and saying 'Namaste'. Hindus believe everyone has God within them. 'Namaste' is a Sanskrit word which means "I bow to the divine in you".

Namaste is putting both the hands together in greeting.

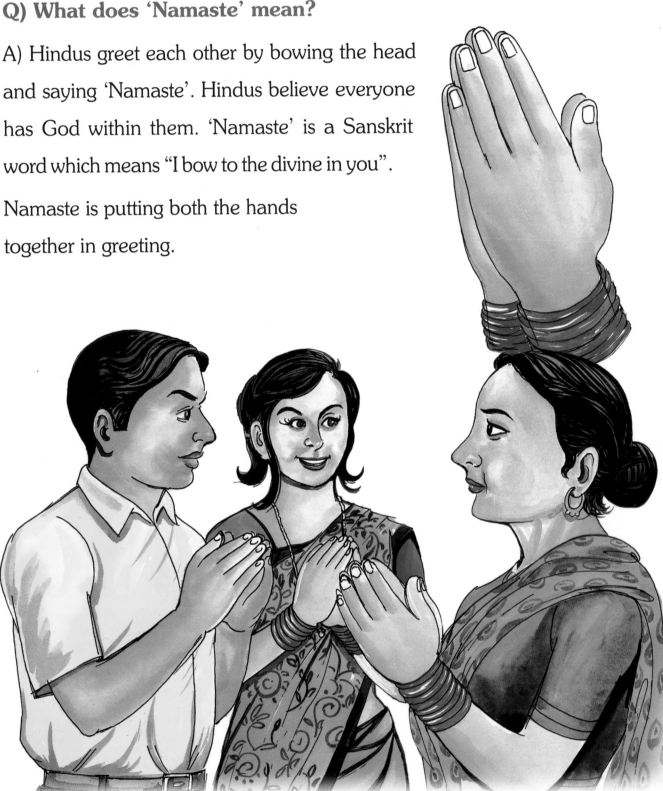

Q) What is the attitude of Hinduism towards other religions?

A) The essence of Hinduism is tolerance. The Rig Veda says: "Truth is one; the wise call it by many names." This alone shows that even so many years ago, Hinduism preached acceptance of other faiths humbly. Hindus consider that all holy trails lead to God; it is just that different names and ways to reach the same goal have developed over time! Respect and peaceful co-existence with other religions is the center of Hinduism. Tolerance of other religions as well an attitude towards peaceful co-existence has allowed Hinduism to survive in spite of centuries of invasions and attacks!

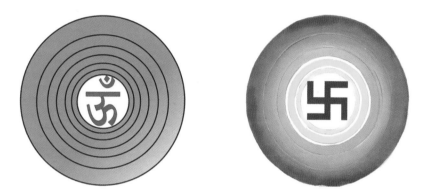

Q) Why do some say Hinduism is not a religion in the conventional sense?

A) Actually, Hinduism is not a religion in the conventional sense. Why? Well, Hinduism has no rigid rules to bind one with God. In fact anyone can be a Hindu if he follows the code of life or Dharma. In Hinduism, its spread does not come by force, but by gentle choice. Hinduism says that the divine is within each one of us and it is for us to recognize HIM and follow the true path. Hinduism allows an individual to choose personally which way is the correct way to be one with God. It even allows you to question it if you feel something is wrong and work towards fixing it! You know why that is possible? Because Hinduism has no founder! So it grows and adapts with time accepting and seeking the most effective channels leading to spiritual paths forever.

Respect for Creation

When you read about Hinduism, it is quite clear that even millions of years ago, respect for everything created by God was very important. Maybe that is why, Hinduism created so many Gods and Goddesses! There were tree gods, herb gods, river goddesses, sky gods and animal gods. Naturally, no one wanted to hurt or destroy divinity. So, we were taught to respect nature's gifts this way! What a better way to preserve environment? Come to think of it, preservation or safe-guarding of nature is preservation of the human race too. How is that? Well, if we preserve rivers, trees and atmosphere, we assure our own survival because if these things disappear, life will not be too good, right? Imagine, having no water to drink, no shade to sit under and no atmosphere to protect us from the sun! I really wish, today, millions of years later, we do not have to hear words like punctured ozone layers, vanishing forests and depleting water sources. Nor we wish to see humans fighting with each other, seeing only the demons within and not the Gods within each one of us. Let us sincerely work towards peaceful co-existence for everything that exists, respecting God's creation.